BARBARA LOBO

ENVIRONMENTAL EDUCATION:

A NEW LEARNING PATHWAY

ISBN: 979-8-218-81888-3

Editorial and research content: **Barbara Lobo**
Cover image: Canva/ Barbara Lobo

Environmental Education: A New Learning Pathway
LOBO, Barbara

1st. Edition
September 2025

I dedicate this book to everyone who wants a better, preserved, diverse, and happy world.

"I only feel angry when I see waste. When I see people throwing away things we could use."

Mother Teresa

Table of Contents

PREFACE

Writing this book about environmental education has been a privilege, as this field has remained central to my professional life for over two decades. Educating others has been a source of profound satisfaction and purpose.

After completing my Master's degree in Health and Environmental Sciences in 2004, I began teaching at a prestigious university in Brazil, marking the beginning of my career in environmental sciences. Although I was new to academia, I was passionate about inspiring others through my enthusiasm for environmental issues. I continue teaching environmental subjects today, now in the United States.

Environmental education was among my first courses when I began teaching higher education students in Environmental Management. In that moment, I realized my career path had found its true direction.

Driven by my passion for education, I pursued a doctorate in educational sciences, a decision that began a journey I continue today. I firmly believe that education has the power to transform social realities.

This book presents a comprehensive examination of environmental education, exploring its role as a bridge between individuals and society. It positions environmental education as a crucial component of modern curricula, particularly relevant to our contemporary challenges.

The book reflects on the evolution of environmental education over recent decades, exploring how schools and teachers can contribute to the effective teaching-learning process. I draw upon insights from researchers, philosophers, and scientists whose work informs this field.

There is an urgent need to rethink both the theory and pedagogical practice of environmental education. This reassessment is essential if we are to expand each individual's capacity to contribute to planetary well-being through everyday actions that will ultimately shape humanity's future. Schools serve as primary venues for this education, with teachers acting as facilitators between curriculum and student learning.

We must also recognize the importance of public policies as vital links between citizens' duties and rights in creating a more sustainable society.

Finally, this book explores collective consciousness and popular participation as integral components of environmental education. I examine the relationships between individuals and their communities, between people and their environment, promoting collaborative actions toward a more just, equitable, preserved, and flourishing world.

To change the world, we must first transform ourselves. Environmental awareness offers a powerful starting point for this transformation, ensuring that future generations inherit a healthier, more beautiful, and better-preserved world in which to live harmoniously.

ACKNOWLEDGEMENTS

Above all, I thank God. Lord, You are good all the time!

From the depths of my heart, I owe immense gratitude to my husband, Alberto Lobo. He has supported me with everything I needed to pursue my path as a writer.

I would especially like to thank my children, Luiza and Gabriel, for being my greatest loves ever. I thank my daughters-in-law, Rafaela—mother of my lovely grandchildren—and Paige, for being part of my family and loving my children.

I am also deeply grateful to my mother for her unwavering support since the day I was born.

Finally, to my beloved grandchildren, Tyler and Mia, I dedicate this work as a legacy. May it inspire you to cherish and protect our environment, ensuring a sustainable future for generations to come.

I. INTRODUCTION

The relationship between education and environmental education is central to the development of this book. It is not possible to understand the process of environmental education without recognizing the educational system as an ally in environmental teaching and learning, aimed at creating a better planet on which to live.

Maintaining a healthy environment is one of the necessary conditions for quality of life. It is essential to plan education as a system where environmental education is an integral part, not separate from it. To ensure the preservation and conservation of species, environmental education is consolidating as a pathway capable of making people aware of how to live on a balanced planet, using natural resources through sustainable actions.

There is a need to expand public engagement through efforts to raise the awareness level of all Earth's inhabitants. It is vital to stimulate environmental education in the process of environmental preservation and in addressing the climate crisis, which has affected all of humanity and caused environmental imbalance and destruction on our planet.

In light of the environmental crisis, increasing industrialization, and rising production and consumption, we recognize the need to discuss education, environmental education, sustainable development, and public participation. Additionally, we must examine the roles of schools and educators in the teaching-learning process aimed at protecting and preserving nature. These elements are crucial allies in maintaining the balance that our environment requires.

An important objective of this book is to discuss key issues in environmental education to understand its significance in various aspects of our lives: in the school environment, in society, in public policies, and throughout history.

Chapter 1, "Education: Starting a Discussion on Teaching vs. Learning," explores education and its relationship to the teaching-learning process. Education is the pathway to human development, building upon the experiences individuals bring from their environment. Through education, individuals can construct their realities, solve problems, and participate in society, becoming better people and creating a better world for all.

Chapter 2, "Economic Development, Problems and Paradigmatic Crisis," examines economic and social development, among other issues, that influence the educational process. The chapter discusses the paradigmatic crisis and its influences as the backdrop to economic development, highlighting the processes of education and public participation as fundamental elements for achieving truly sustainable development.

Chapter 3, "Cartesian Paradigm View: A Discussion," explores the impact of the Cartesian method on humanity's relationship with the environment. It demonstrates how individualistic and disconnected actions and thoughts have emerged as one of the causes of environmental imbalance. The chapter illustrates that in just a few centuries, while humans have advanced economically, this "development" has simultaneously put humanity at risk and led to the destruction of numerous species.

Chapter 4, "Educational Policies as Instruments for Critical Reflection," explores how policies can serve as a basis for reflection, positioning education as an ally in human development and as an important instrument of social transformation.

Chapter 5, "Sustainability Policies," highlights the importance of formulating public policies for the sustainability of our planet.

Chapter 6, "Adult Teaching-Learning," emphatically discusses learning from the perspective of andragogy, which is defined as the art and science of guiding adults through the teaching-learning process.

Chapter 7, "Environmental Education: A Pathway," demonstrates that the importance of environmental education extends beyond merely understanding and acting on ecological problems. It emphasizes establishing a cause-and-effect relationship between degradation processes and the dynamics of social systems.

Chapter 8, "A Brief Walk Through Environmental Education Over History," presents the development of environmental education throughout the years, exploring various summits and agreements. It includes the concept of sustainable development as a global discussion point among most nations worldwide.

Chapter 9, "Critical Reflection on Environmental Education," explores how critical reflection generates praxis, the cycle of action-reflection-action. This chapter discusses the role of education in forming citizenship, preparing individuals to demand their rights and fulfill their duties.

Chapter 10, "Environmental Education at School," demonstrates the school's role as a crucial instrument in forming citizens' awareness about the environment. This chapter presents practical content for constructing the teaching-learning relationship of environmental education integrated into the school curriculum. It emphasizes that the school is where learning occurs and that education is the primary pathway to transform social reality. The chapter concludes that if we desire a better planet, we must utilize school spaces as an interface between students and the environment.

Chapter 11, "Environmental Education and Popular Participation," explores various approaches to increase social engagement with environmental issues. It discusses strategies such as fostering a cohesive collective consciousness and promoting united mobilization.

Environmental education is crucial in building collective awareness regarding environmental preservation. This book emphasizes concepts and practices that highlight the importance of integrating environmental education into public education policies, with schools serving as the focal point where teachers, students, and society come together. Public participation is absolutely vital. Individuals must engage actively in this process. Only through such engagement can we achieve a planet that finds and maintains equilibrium — what we want for future generations.

Finally, Chapter 12, "Toward a Transformative Future: Environmental Education as Catalyst for Global Change," synthesizes the book's central themes and presents environmental education as a transformative practice that goes beyond individual awareness to foster systemic change. It explores the concept of environmental education as praxis, emphasizing the development of "ecological citizens" who understand the interconnections between environmental and social justice issues and possess the skills for democratic environmental action.

1. EDUCATION: STARTING A DISCUSSION ON TEACHING vs. LEARNING

"There is a causal relationship between education and poverty: the absence of the former determines social immobility. The presence of the latter becomes preponderant for performance in the educational learning coefficient index" (Amorim & Lobo, 2016).

This chapter discusses education and its relationship to teaching-learning. Education is the way to build human development combined with the experiences that each individual brings from their environment. Our environments help shape us, and make us who we are. Through education, individuals can build their realities and solve their problems, creating a better society as well as better people.

We believe in an education aimed at forming critical, reflective, and active citizens in the world in which they live. We are not entirely products of the environment, nor do we inherit all our behavior genetically (Piaget, 1959). We are the combination of these two elements. In fact, Piaget recognizes the importance of the environment in the construction of knowledge.

We must reflect on different types of education systems to understand which pathway will be able to lead us to the reality about ourselves. This pathway must be based on values that we believe in, such as freedom, autonomy, and dialectical criticism. Otherwise, if we don't understand education as a means of giving us total independence over ourselves, we are subject to being commanded by a regulated, mechanical, and rigid system.

According to Freire (1970) on the banking concept of education, this process becomes an act of deposit, in which the students are the depositories, and the teacher is the depositor. Students, instead of communicating, patiently receive, memorize, and repeat.

In banking education, we find an oppressive, static, controlled process. This education method makes students into objects.

According to Freire (1970), in this system people are archived by the lack of creativity, capacity for transformation, and knowledge. Apart from research, apart from interactive praxis, individuals cannot be truly human. Knowledge arises only through invention and reinvention, through the restless, impatient, continuous, and hopeful research that human beings carry out into the world, with the world, and with each other.

If we seek an education capable of fostering emancipatory learning, we must work in favor of dialogue, through pedagogical practice oriented towards the teaching-learning relationship, where the student is the builder of knowledge mediated by the teacher. This action is quite different from the banking education method.

On the other hand, liberating education consists of acts of cognition, not transfers of information (Freire, 1970). According to Freire, "those truly committed to liberation must reject the banking concept in its entirety, adopting instead a concept of women and men as conscious beings, and consciousness as consciousness intent upon the world."

Fernández (1991) argues that the learning process takes place at four levels: organism, body, intelligence, and desire. One cannot speak of this process by excluding any one of them. In an orthodox view of the learning process, we consider only conscious aspects of the product of intelligence, leaving aside the body and affections. The current view is very different. The degree of affection between student and teacher becomes very important for the success of the relationship; the degree of bond between the two becomes the essential element for the development of learning, not forgetting the four levels of association.

The human being, in order to learn, has to put into play their inherited organism, their constructed body, their intentionally constructed intelligence, and the architecture of desire. The desire is not originally theirs, but another's learned desire (Amorim & Lobo, 2016).

The matrix of the learning process is playful, and its root is corporeal (Fernández, 1991). Its creativity is linked through intelligence that is irrevocably associated with sexual desire and is assimilated through balance (Amorim & Lobo, 2016). Thus, learning would be, above all, linked to instinct. The fractures that can be verified in this process are associated with instinctive mechanisms.

Knowledge cannot be acquired directly in a block (Fernández, 1991). The teacher transmits their knowledge through teaching. Each piece of information then needs a corresponding emblem. Through symbols we transmit both knowledge and ignorance. We do not transmit knowledge, but signals. These will be absorbed by the learner, then reproduced or decoded.

Learning is not innate. It is external at first, because only the other has it. Therefore, we should know a little about the other who learns. We must have an affective relationship with them. This relies on the teaching and not necessarily the teacher. In the first years of our lives, this can be the parents or any strong ties, whether kin, or not. We can only learn when we allow ourselves to learn. This means we will only learn from a teacher when we grant them the trust and right to teach (Amorim & Lobo, 2016).

For learning, it is up to the school to have as a priority the relationships between student and student, as well as student and teacher, understanding that the teacher acts as a facilitating agent of the learning that takes place from these relationships.

The development of learning is based on the spontaneous content of students, especially in the first years of teaching. From this perspective, the teacher must have enough pedagogical ability to explore the concepts that the student brings and that are defined within the Zone of Actual Development. The Zone of Actual Development is understood as a region belonging to the human being where it considers that each individual can perform tasks alone — this means without anyone's help.

To enrich the relationship between teaching and learning, it is important to know about the Zone of Proximal Development (ZPD), which was a concept created by Lev Vygotsky for his theory of learning and development. According to him, ZPD means the space between what the student can do without adult assistance and what they can do with adult guidance.

Vygotsky understood learning as an internal construction from an external operation. To the extent that the subject internalizes, they learn, and modify their perceptions of things, their way of seeing the world, also modifying their ability to solve problems, that is, their superior psychological functions (Amorim & Lobo, 2016).

According to Vygotsky's theory, we can only understand the individual in terms of their personal territory and their history. This historical-cultural-territorial perspective is based on the development of the higher functions. These typically human functions are: attention, abstract thinking, voluntary behavior, imagination, memory, and the Zone of Potential Development, called by Vygotsky the Zone of Proximal Development. This shifts the meaning of the term to:

what the individual may be able to do will depend on their surroundings (Amorim & Lobo, 2019).

According to Souza, more emphatically, a child's learning has a fundamental basis in their own environment. This place where the child's intellectual development is ensured is called the family (qtd. in Amorim & Lobo, 2019). In the transmission of family cultural heritage, the school has a leading role. In fact, we can consider that both the school and the family are environments that contribute to the learning process. In the absence of one of these two instances, the child's relationship with learning is compromised in terms of quality. That can certainly be an object of development throughout the teaching process, through the signs, symbols, and cultural heritage absorbed through their own human development.

Jung (2000) goes further regarding the environment. According to him, independent of the self-constructed individual, there is a collective unconscious. The collective unconscious forms the subterranean cultural process, that is, everything we don't see: codes of values, ethics, morals, and honor.

According to Lawson (2001) regarding the principles of brain learning, he says that learning is a natural function of the brain: the brain works for its survival. It is naturally not prepared for formal, institutional, and standardized teaching.

Learning is best achieved when many domains — cognitive, affective, and psychomotor — are simultaneously introduced. According to the researcher above, new learning must be relevant: if the brain, consciously or unconsciously, perceives that the teaching is irrelevant, the potential to learn decreases. Emotions are clearly an important factor in student motivation: the brain is naturally and intrinsically motivated to learn.

The most important factor in generating equal opportunities among individuals is education. It is one of the few public policies that has been proven to be efficient, capable of increasing social mobility, and allowing for a more equitable distribution of income. Effective public educational policies must take into account all forms of social infrastructure. There is no individualized psychosocial development.

Human beings grow with the environment, with their peers, with their family, and with their community.

Amorim and Lobo (2016) recognize the importance of education externalities in any society that seeks its own development. According to them, it is difficult to holistically address all externality processes arising from the education system. However, it becomes unquestionable, through vast literature, that the process exists; that is, education positively influences the life of any human community on the planet.

According to Moretti (2004), higher levels of education are associated with high rates of productivity, not only for those who have acquired it but also for their co-workers. The processes of active production in the construction of citizenship are correlated with levels of education (Dee, 2004; Milligan, Moretti, and Oreopoulos, 2004). Higher levels of education are associated with a lower incidence of crime and corruption (Lochner and Moretti, 2004). The democratization of access to education is associated with better health outcomes for the population, which in turn is correlated with lower average assistance costs for the state (Currie and Moretti, 2003). Higher levels of education for parents typically reflect higher levels of education for their children.

All these findings, along with others not addressed here, culminate in higher wages with guaranteed public and private returns. Investment in human capital, therefore, becomes essential for the economic growth of any state, country, or nation.

Now that education as a teaching system has been explained from early childhood, we can understand how adults create their relationship with learning. Going a little beyond the school-learning relationship, we take into account that learning occurs before it, especially during, and, above all, after. This brings reflection on the future we want when the environmental issue becomes a fundamental part of the individual's life, where learning about the environment should be a recurring agenda, inside and outside of school.

In conclusion, a preserved environment is the happy result of an educational system oriented toward it.

2. ECONOMIC DEVELOPMENT, PROBLEMS AND PARADIGMATIC CRISIS

This chapter discusses how economic and social development, among other issues, influence the educational process. The paradigmatic crisis and its influences are discussed as the background to economic development, thus pointing to the processes of education and popular participation as fundamental elements for truly sustainable development.

Society is complex, and crisis circumstances are characterized by the most diverse social segments. The existing development model has proven ineffective in overcoming today's major challenges. Therefore, what occurs is a paradigmatic crisis. Education is pointed to as a solution.

The crisis that plagues education systems across the planet is clear. It has been manifesting itself, fundamentally, in an erosion process that, from the weakening of the bond between school and economic and social development, led to massification, lack of quality, disinvestment, demotivation, and devaluation of teachers.

This perception coincides with the crisis of the structuring paradigm of the school, whose validity collapsed from the moment when industrial society began to give way to a new economic and social organization whose contours are not yet completely defined, although the prevalence of information and knowledge over traditional industries already seems evident.

According to Vasconcellos (2002), the traditional, conservative, and reductionist paradigm focuses on beliefs that can be subdivided into three areas: simplicity, stability, and objectivity. The belief in simplicity proposes the separation of the smallest part to be analyzed and classified in order to understand the complex whole and seek the cause-and-effect relationship. Therefore, there are causal and linear relationships. The belief in stability proposes that the world is invariable, determined, and reversible. Thus, one can know, predict, and control phenomena. As for objectivity, explanation is sought through experimentation and/or empirical verification with quantifiable results.

According to Candau (1995), criticism of the traditional paradigm became more decisive in the 1950s and 1960s, carried out in light of the perspective of the New School movement. In this conception, in which the student becomes the center of the educational/formative process, the educator-student relationship assumes an eminently subjective, affective, and individualizing character. For this educational perspective, the teaching methodology should focus on the process of acquiring attitudes, such as human warmth, empathy, and unconditional positive regard. The teaching methodology is then privatized because personal, interpersonal, and integral growth are unrelated to the socio-economic and political conditions in which they take place.

From the 1960s, the so-called technicist pedagogy, which in many respects confirms the traditional paradigm, expanded, especially in Brazil.

The technicist tendency subordinates education to society, having as its function the preparation of labor for industry. The industrial and technological society establishes the economic, social, and political goals; education trains students with behaviors to adjust to these goals.

At the end of the 1960s, relations between education and society began to be emphatically highlighted. This is especially due to the contributions of Marxist authors such as Althusser, Baudelot, and Establet. These authors situate the capitalist division of labor as both a starting and arrival point in relation to the explanation of the role of the school, and also due to the studies of Bourdieu and Passeron that emphasize the processes used by the school as instruments of reproduction of the dominant culture (Silva, 1990).

Since then, a group of educators, called progressives, among whom Paulo Freire stands out for sustaining a dialectical conception of education in which educators and students learn together, seeking continuous improvement in a dynamic relationship that integrates theory and practice (Freire, 1999), have collaborated so that there would be a clearer awareness of the socio-political determinants of education.

It is a fact that the multiplication of educational problems has contributed to the growth of collective consciousness, as well as to the increase in questions about the relationship between humans and society and about the disintegration of knowledge from economics, ecology, sociology, and biology, in the sense of the approximation of natural, social, and educational sciences.

However, this awakening of collective consciousness has not yet been reflected in significant changes in the direction of government policies and individual lifestyles.

The criticisms also point to the imitative and inappropriate nature of the development formulas transferred from industrialized countries to poor countries with disastrous consequences.

According to Morin & Kern (1995), Buarque (1990), and Correia de Andrade (1993), imitative growth is one of the main mistakes in the construction of a new conception of development, as well as a sign of poor development.

Attempting to replicate the path of industrialized countries entails high social and environmental costs. These costs include the deepening of social inequality and cultural dependence, which, according to the authors above, are structural evils from which others unfold.

Furtado (1996) demonstrates the fallacies of the idea of economic development and the impossibility of its universalization. He demystifies the doctrine that poor countries have the possibility of achieving the living standards of rich countries as long as they follow their models and development recommendations.

The author shows that this goal is unachievable, since the costs would be very high and that any attempt to generalize it would lead to civilizational collapse, endangering the survival of the human species. He states that this idea of development has been used to lead poor countries to accept sacrifice, legitimizing destruction and justifying forms of dependence that reinforce the predatory character of the productive system.

Gonçalves (2002) warns of the need to analyze the meaning of what development is — which means to develop, to break the involvement of men and women among themselves and with the earth, with plants, and with animals, to make them free from it, so that it can be appropriated.

Thus, Gudynas (1992) exposes that current development postures require a critical approach. There is no renunciation of the old paradigm of development by economic growth, but rather, it is adjusted to a new dimension. The dissemination of a new neoliberal policy, which emphasizes the market as a privileged scenario of social relations, is also generating its own policies.

In recent decades, the impacts on educational policies, thinking about education, and the role played by the school in contemporary society, especially in developing areas, have been emerging.

The formation of alliances between the government, civil society, and the private sector to propose programs to combat social exclusion and its direct relationship with the educational process has been occurring since then.

According to Lacerda (2012), contradictory and exclusionary pedagogical practices are discussed, aimed at technical pedagogy or neutral skills, or at relationships between education and various semiotic production practices.

It is urgent to emphasize that the paradigms of education, and education itself, are not the exclusive properties of the school; therefore, ideas, knowledge, and initiatives have multiplied regarding the educational role of the city, institutions, and society.

3. CARTESIAN PARADIGM VIEW: A DISCUSSION

The existence of the human species is immersed in a crisis that can be seen in economic, religious, political, and social aspects, and that endangers the future of humankind.

According to Peccei and Ikeda (1984), the self-destructive madness of human beings seems to be limitless. Anything that pleases the ego is superior to consideration of the consequences of our actions. The struggle for supremacy in fierce competitions to make quick profits no matter the cost or the possibility of breaking ethical standards is put ahead of environmental considerations. Humans become increasingly self-centered and renounce nature.

In a few centuries, humans have destroyed and endangered countless animal and plant species. Cities, metropolises, and megalopolises were born, justified by development. According to Toynbee (1974), humans have violated and destroyed nature in all parts of the world through technological advancement and demographic explosion.

Science and technology are dynamic today. This dynamism is due to the Industrial Revolution and Cartesian principles. The mastery of nature by humans has relied on the costs of slavery to an artificial and inadequate environment. Humans dare to enjoy their artificial creation in order to seek happiness.

A human life is necessarily interdependent. It is our collective responsibility to share in the construction of universal harmony. However, this way of thinking about the relationship with the environment is fairly recent.

In the 17th century, René Descartes proposed the Cartesian paradigm in his work "Discourse on the Method." This conception introduced a conservative and dominant model that advocates rationalization, fragmentation, and a linear view of science, which consequently influenced education as well.

Civilization, especially in the West, as formulated by Bacon and Descartes, leads to unknown paths. Technology and science become imperative, accentuating ambition and perpetual growth. This behavioral and existential formula generates an identity crisis that creates a broken link in the human-nature relationship. Humans lose the notion of existence and move toward a mechanical notion of being. Detachment from nature and unmeasured affection for reason and technique, driven by Cartesian thought, make them predators and explorers.

According to La Torre (1993), nature opposes this binary view and its defeat turns into the defeat of humanity when it pursues absolute power. In turn, paradigms of masculine dominance are created. These ultimately weaken the human-nature relationship and permeate all spheres of Western civilization.

Capra (1982) presents the same ecofeminist vision when he says that Mother Earth has been offering all her riches for the delight of science and technology, coinciding with these masculine views toward women.

With Descartes comes the synthesis of the anthropocentric view. In Western rationality, this begins to guide human attitudes. According to Capra (1982), this overvaluation of the rational being makes humans disconnect from the collective and intuitive senses, proper to the feminist conception. This in turn causes a loss of understanding of the relationship with the environment. Nature is then considered an exploitable object.

Cultural and social evolution cause the loss of biological and ecological references. Intellectual development, scientific, and technological knowledge depart from wisdom and ethics. These freeze, as if they were complete in themselves. Rational and intellectual progress becomes alarming in the face of possible self-extermination (Capra, 1982).

The change in human actions implies a change in ethics. To conceive a new action that does not include the environment as worthy of rights and duties is to remain stuck in the Cartesian paradigm (Jonas, 1995).

For the author above, the desecration of nature and civilization develop together. Both rebel against the elements. The first, by penetrating them and violating their creatures; and the second, in the fallout from the resultant collapse of social systems and civic life.

In their concept of progress, humans mistake the powers of the natural elements, as if they were in no way threatened. With a technical-scientific theory of domination, they believe that everything can be controlled rationally. This uncommitted relationship with nature creates an anthropocentric culture, and nature, unknown and feared, languishes, without the need for care (Jonas, 1995).

Also according to the author above, anthropocentric ethics characterize all non-human objects as having no relevance; traditional ethics are anthropocentric and humans are seen in their condition as an essence, meant to be present in the world and not as objects of transformation; and all the relationships faced by human beings in human-to-human relationships are worthy of ethical and moral judgment, but this judgment does not apply to the human-nature relationship.

However, more modern thought introduces new elements. All these changes impose on ethics the dimension of responsibility. The first and greatest change is the vulnerability of nature. This vulnerability makes humans responsible for the biosphere (Jonas, 1995).

In times past, technology was used simply to meet human needs. Nowadays, technology has an infinite impulse aiming at increasing dominance over things and over humans themselves. According to Jonas (1995), humans are increasingly the product of what they produce. For him, there is no self-contradiction in the idea that humanity ceases to exist. An imperative that perfectly fits the new style of human actions is that the effects of these actions are compatible with the permanence of human life on Earth.

Education brings the Newtonian-Cartesian view, and mechanistic determinism becomes a form of utilitarian and functional knowledge. In this dominant conservative model that accompanied humanity and education until much of the 20th century, training was introduced as a formative model.

In this concept, a conservative approach emerged, based on Cartesian - Newtonian rationality, and an innovative approach that sought to meet a vision of complexity, interconnection, and interdependence.

Newtonian science and its mechanistic ideas view nature as a machine that can be explored and manipulated. This perpetuates the path of exploitation of women and nature. The link between women and nature helps grow feminist and ecological movements worldwide (Capra, 1982). This model is completely contrary to the masculine and anthropocentric Cartesian one.

In the 20th century, during the 1970s, training sought to meet the Fordist model of production, proposing the training of professionals to perform a certain task through modeling. Thus, the Industrial Revolution imposed the model of the development of technical competence — creating the paradigm of complexity in professional training necessary to work in various sectors. Training for technical competence included both the academic and business fields with the need to prepare skilled labor for the labor market.

At the beginning of the 21st century, the innovative paradigm emerged with different theories, including systemic, emergent, or complexity theories (Boaventura Santos,1989; Capra,1997, 2002; Morin, 2002).

According to Morin (2002), the perspective of the systemic principle links the knowledge of the parts to the knowledge of the whole, conceiving the relationship of interdependence between them.

The paradigm of complexity aims at overcoming linear logic and proposes a new conception that has totality and interconnection as its articulating axis. Therefore, the seed of a new vision of humans, society, and the world is beginning to emerge (Moraes, 1997, 2004; Morin, 2002; Behrens, 2005a, 2006).

According to Morin (2003), knowing the living system does not imply separating it from its environment, but contextualizing it in this environment, considering all the events and information that pass through it in a relationship of inseparability.

A local modification has repercussions on the whole, and a modification of the whole has repercussions on the parts. In this way, the paradigm of complexity proposes a vision of an undivided person, who participates in the construction of knowledge not only using reason, but also by combining emotions, feelings, and intuitions. It is urgent that the structures of educational functioning include the use of the concepts of inter-, multi-, and transdisciplinary approaches.

This new imperative must be addressed by public policy. It calls for agreement on the lasting effects of the individual for the continuity of human activity in the future. Jonas (1995) understands that leaders have responsibility for today's humanity and the well-being of future generations.

By creating ethical conditions for coexistence in society, good leaders will be contributing to citizens seeking high value outcomes, making them more willing to make sacrifices for the common good.

It is important to emphasize that the objective is not questioning the validity of ethics for its own purposes, but addressing its insufficiency in the face of new human actions, namely, technology and science. That is why an ethics of foresight and responsibility is necessary as new circumstances arise. It is up to the reformulated and holistic ethics to constantly revise and update useful standards of conduct (Jonas, 1995).

According to the same author, human knowledge has given humans scientific forces that need to be regulated by norms. We must establish an ethics that can curb extreme capacities, because ethics exists to contain human actions and regulate human power. Therefore, the new capacities of action require new ethical rules, or perhaps an entirely new ethics.

Two forms of ethics are then distinguished: the simple ethics of duty and responsibility, and a more comprehensive ethics of aspiration. In the ethics of duty are respect for nature, preservation, and responsibility for future generations. In the ethics of aspiration, feelings of beauty, harmony, mystical and fraternal union with nature are considered, as well as the relationship between care and creation (La Torre, 1993).

According to Boff (2000), care means zeal, solicitude, diligence, attention, and good treatment. Thus, nature is not seen as an object of exploitation and domination. There is an ongoing relationship of coexistence. It ceases to be a subject-object relationship and becomes a subject-subject one.

When we consider care, we cease seeing otherness as separate from ourselves. It represents the absolute ethical untouchability. Unity in the human-nature relationship happens when humans strip themselves of the totalizing, centralizing, and exploitative position, and seek a relationship of respect, holistic and mutual responsibility (De Souza, 1996).

According to Boff (2000), one of the great challenges is reconciling the way-of-being-care with the way-of-being-work; these are two complementary dimensions, but understood and experienced in opposite ways. Work is a way to accumulate capital, to achieve conquest of the other, of the world, of nature. On the other hand, the way-of-care springs from feeling, understanding, empathy, and care. And this feminine way of being makes nature Mother and Sister.

This new position does not mean a total abandonment of work or reason, but a form of balanced and harmonious integration with the universe.

The ethics of responsibility associated with the ethics of compassion generates a new understanding of nature. Constructive bonds are formed, in which care is the driving force of action. Reason, in turn, becomes an instrument of ethical distinction, assisting in choices. This new ethic could generate a new way of being in the world and establish a new alliance between reason, compassion, and responsibility (Kösel, 1957, as cited in Boff, 1999).

4. EDUCATIONAL POLICIES AS INSTRUMENTS FOR CRITICAL REFLECTION

Critical reflection generates praxis, the cycle of action-reflection-action. The role of education is to form citizens, preparing people to demand their rights and fulfill their duties. It is up to education to contribute to social participation and representativeness, influencing the formulation of public policies and the construction of the culture of democracy.

According to Guimarães (2000), two lines of proposals for education stand out: one linked to the popular interests of emancipation, social equality, and better quality of life, and another that acts in the interests of capital, following market logic, defended by the dominant groups. It is during this moment of restructuring of the world order in the neoliberal context that it is fundamental to define the type of education, demonstrating whether it points to the emancipatory popular proposal or if it is compatible with the process of social exclusion.

According to Pelicioni and Philippi Jr. (2002), humanity needs a new project that considers the question of the universality of human beings within the historical process, establishing the ethics of the promotion of life. This requires reflections and actions on inequalities, poverty, exclusion, practices, and consumer relations. This also presupposes the reconstruction of paradigms and the relations of humankind with society, requiring continuous reflection.

The critical knowledge of reality, which is acquired in its unfolding, does not by itself bring about change, but however, it represents a step toward overcoming it (Freire, 1992). Pedagogical praxis, as an educational dimension of political action, is constituted by creative action against the relations of domination currently in force in society, which produce social misery, social exclusion, and are ultimately responsible for a possible planetary crisis (Guimarães, 2000).

Educational policy must not lose sight of the complex challenges that arise and, consequently, must maintain the values of autonomy, citizenship, and social justice as the basic principles of education (Reigota, 2003).

According to Bell and Stevenson (2006, p.11):

> "Educational policy studies tend to take one of three forms: the development of analytical models through which policies can be analyzed and interpreted; the analysis of a number of policy-related issues; and the analysis of policy criticism."

Research in educational policy should be based on broader projects and roles in which social problems are managed, allowing researches through research to categorize, professionalize, and restrict themselves to specific problems (Ball, 1995). In this context, epistemological development in education works politically and is strictly implicated in the practical management of social problems.

Indeed, research in educational policy uses various positions, concerns, and diverse models in relation to the methods and processes of reform and in relation to the traditions and practices of the human sciences. Educational crises are manifestations of historical, structural, and ideological contradictions in educational policies.

A challenge for educational policy is the development of a critical theory of recognition that identifies and sustains the versions of cultural policy combined with a social policy of equality, based on new intellectual tasks and related practices.

It is urgent to emphasize that the post-structuralist perspective seeks to determine the limitations of descriptive and pluralistic approaches to educational policies: in these, the sense of power circulates among the different stakeholders. "Marxist approaches focus on the role of the state and the generation of policies as a reflection of the divergences of power between the economy and political agents" (Ball, 2011, p. 156). The post-structuralists emphasized that the action of the subject is determinant for the understanding of policies and that power, and its possession, are conceived differently by the different agents.

It is necessary to analyze educational policies, understood as text and discourse (Ball, 2011). Based on Foucault, Ball understands that, in practice, actors translate policies into a variety of discourses; however, some will place themselves in the context of domination over others.

The conception of policy based on pluralism is different from the representation that Marxists make of it. Pluralists emphasize an unarticulated set of centers of power and influence, with the State being only one. The confrontation with criticism is emphasized both in the approaches of post-structuralist and pluralistic educational policies. Policy aggregates the meanings of practice and thus demonstrates the interpenetration between domination and resistance, resulting, at certain moments, in the ambivalence of discourses (Ball, 2011).

In short, only through education developed from solid political, conceptual, philosophical, and ideological bases can new and positive approaches to educational development be implemented. However, reflections and discussions of the theoretical and methodological aspects of educational policies are necessary to drive qualitative advances in education.

5. SUSTAINABILITY POLICIES

A development strategy should not be based simply on the predatory form of the use of nature without considering significant compensation for the loss of natural capital that occurs (Cavalcanti, 2002).

According to the same author, what can be advanced in the formulation of public policies for sustainability is that the real environmental problem consists precisely of maintaining the capital of nature, using its stocks in a healthy manner, without overloading the functions of supply, source (resources), and absorption or disposal of ecosystem waste.

Sustainable development policies, since their emergence, have always meant, irrefutably, some form of environmental degradation; the economic process must use nature in a more durable, sober, and healthy way than has been the practice to date (Roegen, 1974, as cited in Cavalcanti, 2002).

The discourse of development regarding the increase in per capita value, which would effectively result in growth, is questionable. What is expected is that this supposed growth will lead to the reduction or eradication of poverty.

According to Cleveland (2002), the problem becomes more acute when it is empirically verified that increasing amounts of natural capital have been needed to produce a unit of resource for society, as is evidenced by studies on scarcity (Cavalcanti, 2002).

Opting for sustainability means adopting a guideline to conserve more natural capital for future generations. This implies accepting a philosophy of finitude and self-restraint, which is not easy to reconcile with globalized attitudes of consumption (Cavalcanti, 2002).

An important principle of policy formulation for sustainability is to have a consistent information system to measure the economic performance of a country or region. According to Viola (1996), in a sustainable society, progress must be understood through quality of life (health, longevity, maturity, psychological well-being, education, a clean environment, community spirit, intelligently enjoyed leisure, and so on), and not by material consumption.

Government policy for sustainability means an orientation of public actions motivated by the recognition of the fundamental ecological limitation of resources, without which no human activity can be carried out. According to Roegen (1971), the strategic problem is to find the sustainable metabolic flow which can increase societal well-being without causing damage to environmental functions and services; in other words, the level of the social product must be maintained, as well as the quality of the natural environment and the quality of life.

6. ADULT TEACHING-LEARNING

To carry out an education process, it is necessary to create a concept of general interest. This is due to the multidimensionality of education for active citizenship. In other words, we need to connect our knowledge base with the education system to create public interest and public participation. A more active construction in society in terms of learning and applicability of this in contexts beyond school is how education should work.

According to Loureiro et al. (2002), paradigm shifts require changes in attitude. The process of participation is only realized through conscious acceptance of its cause. Access to information, especially for more excluded social groups, can promote the behavioral changes necessary to enable more action oriented toward the general interest. Well-informed citizens, by considering themselves as relevant actors, are more able to pressure authorities, as well as to motivate themselves to actions of co-responsibility and community participation (Jacobi, 1999).

This possibility also appears when the process of educating becomes an interaction between teacher and student, according to Freire (1987, p.68):

> "The educator is no longer the one who only teaches, but the one who also learns through the dialogue between them and the student. Both become subjects of the process in which they grow together and in which the arguments of authority are no longer valid."

According to Freire (1989), the object of learning is significant content, related to the experiential contexts of the students. The understanding of new knowledge is facilitated by the dialogical relationship that is established among all participants in the process.

By developing educational praxis through dialogue as a process of reflection and action in the construction of knowledge, it is fundamental to intervene in reality and promote change leading to citizenship. This perspective implies a dialectical movement between the critical unveiling of reality and transformative social action, according to the principle that human beings educate each other and are mediated by the world (Freire, 2002).

For education to be effective, it cannot be isolated, but must be interactive, as Freire stated:

> "From this process comes a knowledge that is critical, because it was obtained in an authentically reflective way, and implies a constant act of unveiling reality, and positioning oneself in it. Knowledge constructed in this way perceives the need to transform the world, allowing the actors to discover themselves as historical beings" (Freire, 1983).

Freire and Knowles provided an important contribution to this form of learning, which is the paradigm for andragogy. Andragogy is defined as the art and science of guiding adults through the teaching-learning process. This methodology varies considerably from traditional pedagogy oriented toward children. (Pacheco et al., 2006)

The word "andragogy" comes from the Greek "andros", which means adult, and "agogos", which means educating. This science aims to help in development and has specific characteristics.

Through andragogy, adults are motivated to learn as they experience that their needs and interests are satisfied. Learning is life-centered, so programs should be focused on life situations rather than academic disciplines.

Andragogy is based on principles that are closely linked with constructivism and social interactionism, considering that adults build their knowledge through internal and external motivations.

According to Gil (2007), the principles that underlie andragogy, based on the constructivist and socio-interactionist approach, highlight the importance of personal issues (desires, interests, and personal history) and social issues (historical-cultural context) for the teaching-learning relationship.

For a better understanding, we present below the principles, according to Gil (2007):

1. **Learner:** the one who is self-directed, which means that they are responsible for their learning and define their educational path.

2. **Need for knowledge:** adults know the real need for knowledge for themselves.

3. **Motivation to learn:** the adult considers external motivations (better work, salary), but also values internal motivations (willingness to grow, self-esteem, recognition, self-confidence, and developing personal potentialities).

4. **Experience:** the educational process is based on the many experiences brought by the student, not only the teacher, and the didactic-pedagogical resources ensure the interest in learning.

5. **Readiness for learning:** the adult becomes available to learn when he/she intends to improve their performance in relation to a certain aspect of their life. Thus, their learning selection is natural and realistic.

Regarding the constructivist approach, according to Piaget (Lima, 2000), knowledge does not consist of copying reality, but of acting on it and transforming it, in order to understand it according to the transformation systems to which these actions are linked. Each person actively builds their understanding of the world through the interaction of their capacities with the environment around them.

Some education experts often consider constructivism as one of the models that best supports teaching (Goulart, 2001).

Despite the importance of constructivism for the construction of knowledge, Vygotsky developed a study on the knowledge resulting from the relationship of the organism with the environment in which it is placed. This model proposes a comprehensive approach capable of describing and explaining higher psychological functions through social interactionism.

According to Vygotsky (Soto, 2005), the socio-interactionist approach puts forward the idea that humans belong to a complex social system in which actions, attitudes, and behaviors are processed, generating knowledge that continues to evolve, receiving feedback that will be processed again and thus perpetuating learning. In this approach, human development takes place in exchanges between social partners, through processes, interaction, and mediation.

Even though these theories, constructivism and socio-interactionism, are focused on the learning of children, many of the concepts, in essence, can be used with adults. This is because the interaction necessary for adult learning requires, above all, imagination and experiences.

Therefore, experience is the richest source for the adult to learn, so the center of the methodology of adult education is the analysis of experiences. Adults have the need to be self-directed, and in this context, the teacher's role is to engage in the process of mutual investigation with students and not just to transmit and evaluate. The integration of theory and practice is fundamental for the construction of knowledge to be acquired. This is especially true regarding experiences focused on the area of industrial safety, which requires beyond technical knowledge, a preventive attitude and the development of autonomy, interaction, and teamwork, in addition to the recognition of leadership. According to Skinner (as cited in Fiorelli, 2001, p. 35-36), "behavior results from the interaction between the individual and the environment".

According to Soto (2005, p. 9): "Education makes the person easy to lead, but difficult to manipulate; easy to govern, but impossible to enslave." Thus, we understand that the ability to exercise essential authentic leadership is fundamental to every human being, so respect must prevail in the context of teaching-learning.

Learning should begin with action-reflection-action. Thus, it should start at home, reach the street and the neighborhood, encompass the community, cover the city, extend beyond the peripheries, rethink the fate of pockets of poverty, penetrate the intimacy of oppressive spaces, reach the peculiarities and regional diversities to integrate the national spaces of education. Observe, participate, analyze, reflect. Repeat.

From the reflection, there is a need to evaluate for decision-making. To evaluate is to make ethical and value judgments, both for those who evaluate and for those who are evaluated.

Ribeiro (1990, p. 47) said the following about evaluation:

> "When considering the task of formulating judgments or valuations as an essential characteristic of the evaluation, the subject who evaluates is faced with the need to clearly define the criteria with which such judgments or valuations should be made. Such evaluation criteria or standards should be reference points that will make it possible to qualify what is proposed to be assessed."

Evaluation is a value judgment on relevant manifestations of reality, with a view to decision-making (Luckesi, 1986).

In conclusion, we perceive a direct link between learning, reflection, and evaluation. Learning is the acquisition of the ability to explain, to teach, to understand, and to critically face new situations (D'ambrosio, 1999). Álvarez Méndez (2002) considers that only when we guarantee learning can we also guarantee evaluation.

7. ENVIRONMENTAL EDUCATION: A PATHWAY

Environmental education, in its concept and intention, holds a position contrary to the model of economic development of the capitalist system. It requires deep knowledge of the philosophy, theory, and history of education, as well as its objectives and principles, since it is an education applied to environmental issues. Its conceptual basis draws from education, environmental sciences, history, social science, economics, and other fields (Pelicioni & Philippi Jr., 2002).

The importance of environmental education is not only about understanding and acting on ecological problems, but rather about establishing a cause-and-effect relationship between degradation processes and the dynamics of social systems. According to Mello and Souza (2000), it suffers from theoretical omissions and the narrow fractionation of its meanings and aims to contribute to the improvement of critical awareness in relation to the ecological crisis.

According to Sorrentino (1995), the complexity of the concept of environmental education influenced the classification of environmental education into four major theoretical-practical categories: conservationist, outdoor education, environmental management, and ecological economy.

Furthermore, Sorrentino explains that the first is present in advanced societies through the actions of entities that defend pristine biophysical nature. The second current is present in the work of former naturalists and educators, in addition to those who seek self-knowledge through contact with nature. Environmental management has strong political implications and is linked to the struggles of social movements. Ecological economy, on the other hand, is inspired by the concept of eco-development, which defends alternative technologies in land treatment, energy use, waste treatment, and other areas.

The objective of environmental education is to contribute to biodiversity conservation, individual and community self-realization, and political and economic self-management, through educational processes that improve the environment and quality of life (Sorrentino, 2005).

Environmental education can be carried out in any organizational space or not. We can identify three different types of environmental education teaching:

1. **Formal environmental education** is characterized by the formal teaching of environmental education, an activity carried out in institutional spaces, composed of a pedagogical plan, with learning objectives and evaluations. It can be concluded that this type of teaching occurs most frequently in school units.

2. Activities carried out in social settings, or public or private institutions, but not registered as educational units, shall be considered **non-formal environmental education**. However, they differ from informal ones because their

socio-educational context is oriented toward environmental awareness with clear objectives.

3. **Informal environmental education** may be considered any type of activity carried out in non-organizational spaces, without connection to any specific teaching method, but which addresses environmental issues informally.

In summary, environmental education must reach all people in the world through permanent action, where participation is the main instrument of action. The focus of the problem is the environment and its crisis, and the solution can be found in collective consciousness about the necessary care in relation to the planet, its genesis, and evolution.

8. A BRIEF WALK THROUGH ENVIRONMENTAL EDUCATION OVER HISTORY

The issues of the environment and environmental education are intertwined throughout history. In the 1960s, the environment was not primarily characterized as a focus of interest in nature preservation or conservation, especially in developed countries. Society was also based on predatory consumption and productivity, although social movements were trying to make something happen.

In the 1970s, the term environment became part of the global discussion, at the heart of the economic crisis that affected most world nations. Environmental education began in view of the tension and pressure of the moment, amid the alarming pace of the environmental tragedy of modernity (Santos, 2000).

In 1972, the United Nations Conference on the Human Environment took place in Stockholm.

Furthermore, the environment became a political interest, and the United Nations Environment Program (UNEP) was established and implemented in 1973. It is interesting to highlight in this period the study called "The Limits to Growth," carried out by the Club of Rome. This document was much criticized because it showed concern for the environmental issue; however, it was alarmingly presented.

In 1977, the Tbilisi Conference (Georgia, former USSR) showed the need for an interdisciplinary approach and for the knowledge and understanding of environmental issues by society as a whole (Pelicioni & Philippi Jr., 2002).

In 1987, according to Pelicioni & Philippi Jr. (2002), the Moscow Conference established guidance and evaluation of actions and goals for the realization of environmental education in all societies on the planet, being currently assumed by both government public policies and entities in the non-governmental sphere.

It is important to emphasize that environmental education was discussed during the

Rio '92 Conference, where the Environmental Education Treaty for Sustainable Societies and Global Responsibility was established, after discussion, suggestion, elaboration, and finally, approval. Diversity was a pertinent theme within this document, establishing a commitment of individual and collective character to sustainability. This occurred as a manifesto for sustainable development of societies. A commitment to environmental education was established after this treaty, becoming an important part of formal education, according to government plans.

In 1997, at the International Conference Environment and Society: Education and Public Awareness for Sustainability held in Greece, the reorientation of education toward sustainability was proposed. At this meeting, it was understood that this concept should cover not only the environment, but also poverty, housing, health, food security, democracy, human rights, and peace, as a moral and ethical imperative, in which traditional knowledge and cultural differences should be respected (Pelicioni, 2000).

In Kyoto, Japan, the Kyoto Protocol was signed in 1997, as a new component of the Convention, which contained, for the first time, a binding agreement that committed northern countries to reduce their emissions. This Protocol committed a number of industrialized nations to reduce their emissions by 5.2% — compared to 1990 levels — for the period 2008-2012. It established three flexibility mechanisms that allowed these countries to comply with emission reduction requirements outside their territories.

According to Greenpeace, projects related to carbon sequestration, nuclear power, large dams, and "clean carbon" did not meet the requirements to receive emission credits under the Clean Development Mechanism (CDM), as it required projects to produce long-term, real, and measurable benefits.

In June 1997, Rio+5 was held. On this occasion, 53 heads of state met in New York to assess the progress made in the five years after Rio '92, in relation to the commitments made at that time, in addition to accelerating the implementation of Agenda 21. At this meeting, the growth of the globalization process, capital markets, and foreign investment was recognized. Lower fertility and population growth rates worldwide were also identified. There were some advances in institutional development, international consensus, public participation, and private sector actions.

On the other hand, among the delays found, attention was drawn to poverty and consumption and production patterns, which remained unsustainably high. Income inequalities had widened between nations and within each of them, as well as environmental degradation, globally (Kranz & Mourão, 1997).

Five years after 1997, the World Summit on Sustainable Development, also known as Rio+10, met in Johannesburg, South Africa. This event brought together government leaders from around the world, as well as significant participation from the productive sector and local and regional authorities.

The main objective was to define objectives and strict deadlines for the effective protection of the environment.

The historical scenario in which this event occurred was very different from the panorama of Rio '92, when the world had just emerged from the Cold War and which had been marked by the need to strengthen international solidarity in combating threats to security, which compromised the effective sustainability of development on a global scale.

The central theme of Rio+10, proposed at the preparatory meetings in 2001, was the search for a new globalization that would ensure equitable and inclusive sustainable development (Vargas, 2002). The World Summit on Sustainable Development Rio+10 focused its discussions on three main themes: government commitments to reduce poverty and protect the environment in poor countries, implement Agenda 21, and transfer resources and technology; parallel meetings to discuss the proposal to convert the energy matrix to ten percent renewable sources and policies to protect biological diversity; and meetings and side events promoted by NGOs to discuss issues such as poverty, the environment, gender issues, and human rights.

"The Future We Want" was the theme of the Rio+20 Conference in 2012 in Rio de Janeiro, Brazil. The United Nations Conference on Sustainable Development, informally called the Rio+20 Summit, was a global meeting where social inequality was discussed with a view to raising the standard of living of humanity.

At the 2012 meeting, world leaders concluded in a final document called "The Future We Want" saying that we should not give up:

> "We are committed to reinvigorating the global partnership for sustainable development that we launched in Rio in 1992. We recognize the need to give new impetus to our cooperative pursuit of sustainable development and are committed to working together with major groups and other stakeholders to address implementation gaps."[1]

---

[1] UN General Assembly, 2012, as cited in Sachs, 2015.

Furthermore, "The Future We Want" reaffirmed the need to achieve sustainable development according to the UN General Assembly:

> "Promoting sustained, inclusive and equitable economic growth, creating greater opportunities for all, reducing inequalities, raising basic standards of living; fostering equitable social development and inclusion; and promoting integrated and sustainable management of natural resources and ecosystems that supports, inter alia, economic, social and human development while facilitating ecosystem conservation, regeneration and restoration and resilience in the face of new and emerging challenges".[2]

In addition, globalization, environmental impacts, and the poor distribution of income were addressed. This discussion highlighted the need to eradicate poverty and change consumption patterns to achieve sustainable development.

---

[2] UN General Assembly, 2012, as cited in Sachs, 2015.

In 2015, New York hosted the Sustainable Development Summit, where the new Sustainable Development Goals (SDGs) and a universal sustainability agenda for 2030 were defined. Ending poverty, protecting the environment, and combating climate change were the specific objectives of this meeting. These narratives had already been on the agenda of discussion in 2000 with the adoption of the Millennium Development Goals (MDGs), which also included the fight against extreme poverty by 2015, as a commitment made by the 191 leaders of the United Nations Member States.

The Paris Agreement, adopted at the 21st Conference of the Parties (COP21) in Paris in 2015, marked a pivotal moment in global climate action. This landmark accord brought together 196 countries in a commitment to limit global temperature rise to well below 2°C above pre-industrial levels, with efforts to limit the increase to 1.5°C. Unlike previous climate agreements, the Paris Agreement established a framework for regular review and strengthening of national commitments over time.

In 2016, Habitat III took place in Quito, Ecuador, establishing the New Urban Agenda. This conference recognized that more than half of the world's population lives in cities, making urban sustainability crucial for environmental protection. The agenda emphasized sustainable urbanization as key to achieving broader environmental and social goals.

Sustainable development is normative, which means that it recommends a set of objectives to which the world must aspire. The nations of the world adopted the SDGs precisely to assist in the future course of the economic and social development of the planet.

In 2019, another major conference in New York discussed climate change. At this meeting, according to the UN, the main goal was to help the world achieve carbon neutrality by 2050. Achieving carbon neutrality means that countries should no longer emit more polluting gases than nature is able to absorb. However, there is alarming chaos in the world that amplifies the climate crisis. The emission of toxic gases being released on a large planetary scale being reduced by 2050 seems ambitious at best.

The urgency of climate action intensified at COP26 in Glasgow in 2021, where nations emphasized the critical need to reach net-zero emissions by 2050. This summit included significant commitments to end deforestation by 2030 and reduce methane emissions by 30% by 2030. The Glasgow Climate Pact explicitly mentioned the need to phase down coal power and inefficient fossil fuel subsidies for the first time in UN climate negotiations.

Stockholm+50, held in Sweden in 2022, commemorated the 50th anniversary of the groundbreaking 1972 Stockholm Conference. This meeting served as a reflection point, acknowledging both the progress made and the accelerated action needed to address environmental challenges. The conference emphasized the interconnection between human well-being and planetary health.

Most recently, COP28 in Dubai in 2023 conducted the first global stocktake of climate progress since the Paris Agreement. This assessment revealed that while some progress had been made, the world remained significantly off track to meet climate goals. The conference marked a historic moment with explicit discussions about transitioning away from fossil fuels in energy systems.

COP29 took place in Baku, Azerbaijan, in November 2024, demonstrating both progress and persistent challenges in global climate cooperation. The conference concluded with developed countries agreeing to provide at least $300 billion annually to developing countries by 2035, tripling the previous target. However, this fell short of the $1.3 trillion that developing nations argued was needed. To address this gap, negotiators established the "Baku to Belém Roadmap to 1.3T" to explore pathways for scaling up climate finance through various mechanisms, including private investment and innovative financing tools.

Looking ahead, COP30 is scheduled to take place in November 2025 in Belém, Brazil, marking a significant moment as the conference will be held in the heart of the Amazon. This location choice is particularly symbolic, representing a powerful reminder of global responsibility to maintain climate targets. By COP30, countries will present the second round of nationally determined contributions, making this conference crucial for assessing and strengthening global climate commitments. Brazil, as the COP30 presidency, plans to launch initiatives focused on forest conservation and sustainable development, representing an opportunity to demonstrate climate leadership while highlighting the critical role of the Amazon rainforest in global climate stability.

In conclusion, we can see that as a democratic practice, environmental education prepares people for the exercise of citizenship through active individual and collective participation, taking into account the socioeconomic, political, and cultural processes that influence it. It requires new strategies to strengthen critical awareness, enabling the population to take social action committed to the reform of the capitalist system.

9. ENVIRONMENTAL EDUCATION: A CRITICAL REFLECTION

Environmental education, when approached through a critical lens, transcends traditional pedagogical boundaries to become a transformative force for social and ecological change. This critical perspective demands that we examine not only what we teach about the environment, but how environmental knowledge intersects with power structures, social justice, and democratic participation.

Unlike conventional environmental education that often focuses on individual behavior change or technical solutions, critical environmental education recognizes that environmental problems are fundamentally social problems. Freire's concept of critical pedagogy, when applied to environmental education, reveals how ecological degradation is intertwined with systems of oppression and social inequality (Guimarães, 1995). This approach challenges learners to question whose voices are heard in environmental decision-making and whose communities bear the greatest burden of environmental harm.

Critical environmental education must center the experiences of marginalized communities who face disproportionate environmental risks. Following Brandão's (1994) framework of popular education, environmental learning becomes most powerful when it emerges from the lived experiences of those most affected by environmental injustice. This means recognizing that indigenous communities, the urban poor, and rural workers often possess essential ecological knowledge that mainstream environmental discourse overlooks.

The dominant environmental narrative often presents nature as separate from human society, obscuring the ways that environmental destruction serves specific economic interests. Critical environmental education exposes how corporate-driven consumption patterns and neoliberal policies accelerate ecological crisis while shifting responsibility to individual consumers (Pelicioni & Philippi Jr., 2002). Students learn to identify and challenge these hegemonic narratives, developing what we might call "ecological consciousness" that connects environmental and social analysis.

Critical environmental education embodies praxis — the integration of reflection and action. This means that environmental learning must move beyond classroom discussions to engage with real environmental conflicts and community organizing efforts. Students and educators participate in environmental justice campaigns, document local environmental problems, and work with community groups to develop solutions that address both ecological and social needs. Through this process, environmental education becomes a tool for democratic participation and social transformation.

The ultimate goal of critical environmental education is not simply environmental literacy, but the development of ecological citizens capable of challenging the structural roots of environmental crisis. This requires an understanding that genuine sustainability cannot be achieved without addressing inequality, racism, and economic exploitation. Environmental educators working from this perspective help learners develop both the analytical tools to understand these connections and the practical skills to work for transformative change.

Critical environmental education recognizes that all education is political, and that environmental education either serves to maintain existing power relations or works to transform them. By connecting local environmental struggles to broader patterns of global inequality, this approach helps learners understand their role as agents of ecological and social change rather than passive recipients of environmental information. This perspective challenges the notion that environmental problems can be solved through technological fixes or individual lifestyle changes alone, instead emphasizing the need for systemic transformation.

In conclusion, critical environmental education offers a pathway toward genuine sustainability by addressing the social roots of environmental crisis. Rather than treating symptoms, this approach works to transform the economic and political systems that drive ecological destruction while building the democratic capacity needed for a just and sustainable future. Through this critical lens, environmental education becomes not just a means of transmitting knowledge about nature, but a powerful tool for social and ecological transformation.

10. ENVIRONMENTAL EDUCATION AT SCHOOL

The worsening of environmental problems necessitates that measures to reduce environmental impacts should be implemented as rapidly as the advance of predatory actions. Among these measures, educational work is undoubtedly one of the most urgent and necessary, because currently most environmental imbalances are related to human behaviors driven by consumerist appeals that generate waste and by the inappropriate use of natural resources, such as soils, water, and forests.

In addition to formulating theoretical proposals, approving laws, and introducing curricular and didactic guidelines in educational systems, it is necessary to have more monitoring and greater support for what happens inside schools, specifically in the classroom space. That is where education truly occurs, whether through significant or small actions.

Society assigns to schools the function of developing certain knowledge considered basic, such as reading, mathematics, and concepts of science, geography, and history. This knowledge is deemed useful for people to enter the workforce and exercise citizenship. In this school context, environmental protection must be integrated. This is where environmental education takes place, through the discussion of environmental preservation beyond the sciences. This topic is also relevant to literature, art, mathematics, philosophy, and other disciplines within the curriculum.

According to Menezes and Iório (1994), ecological themes should be incorporated into this educational environment because they address the relationship between humans and nature, and their study facilitates integration among disciplines such as science, geography, history, and language. Moreover, current issues like pollution, deforestation, and energy production have increasingly gained prominence in the media. This trend allows educators to find relevant examples and problems to illustrate or develop school content. Finally, environmental studies can foster greater contact between the school and the local community, facilitating the interconnection of local, regional, and global realities.

According to Vasconcellos (1997), environmental education requires the presence of reflection in all educational practices. This reflection should focus on three types of relationships: among living beings, between humans and themselves, and among humans and their peers.

Within this context, schools stand out as privileged spaces for implementing activities that foster this reflection. Such activities include both classroom and field experiences, with actions oriented towards projects and participatory processes. These approaches lead to self-confidence, positive attitudes, and personal commitment to environmental protection, all implemented in an interdisciplinary manner (Dias, 1993).

The process of sensitizing the school community promotes initiatives that transcend the school environment. These initiatives reach both the immediate neighborhood where the school is located and the more distant communities where students, teachers, and staff reside. These individuals become potential multipliers of information and activities related to environmental education implemented in the school. Soares (2000) further asserts that strengthening both internal and external school relationships is highly beneficial for environmental conservation, particularly within the school environment.

It is necessary for schools to promote student contact with popular movements, environmental groups, trade unions, and associations that participate in political and social activities. Through this engagement, children and young people can be exposed to possibilities for transformative action, fulfilling the ethical and political functions of education. Without these functions, schools would be devoid of their social meaning (Menezes & Iório, 1994).

According to Dias (1993), work related to environmental education in schools should have the following objectives: raising awareness, promoting behavioral change, encouraging active participation of the population, and enhancing the teacher's role as an agent promoting environmental education. Through this approach, environmental education becomes a continuous and permanent process, with interdisciplinary, globalizing actions that integrate school and community, aiming at environmental protection in harmony with sustainable development.

It is important to recognize that implementing environmental education in schools is an exhaustive task. There are significant challenges in awareness-raising and training activities, in the implementation of projects, and, most importantly, in maintaining and ensuring the continuity of existing programs. Various factors contribute to these challenges, such as:

1. School size
2. Number of students and teachers
3. Teachers' willingness to undergo training
4. The school administration's commitment to implementing environmental projects that alter school routines

In addition to the factors mentioned above and their interactions, other elements can serve as obstacles to the implementation of environmental education. This is because environmental education is not achieved through specific activities alone, but requires a complete paradigm shift. This shift demands continuous reflection and internalization of related values. Consequently, the difficulties faced in implementing environmental education become even more pronounced.

Given the above premises, the effective implementation of environmental education in schools requires an approach that is not hierarchical, aggressive, competitive, or exclusive. Instead, the implementation process should be based on cooperation, participation, and fostering autonomy among all involved parties.

We emphasize that projects imposed by small groups or isolated activities, managed by only a few individuals within the school community, are insufficient to produce the necessary change in mentality. Such limited approaches cannot establish attitudes that transcend the school environment and reach the broader society.

Alternatives should be sought that promote continuous reflection, culminating in a change of mentality. Only in this way is it possible to implement true environmental education in schools. This approach involves activities and projects that are not merely illustrative, but are the result of the entire school community's desire to build a future where one can live in a balanced environment, in harmony with nature, other living beings, and fellow humans.

The strategy for implementing environmental education should be based on an expanded vision that addresses both the curricular aspects of the school and the practical task of transforming the school itself. This transformation should shift the school from being an institution with environmental impact to one that contributes to reducing the city's environmental problems. In this way, the school would become not only an agent of change but also an object of change.

This approach offers several benefits:

1. Environmental education promotes behavioral changes that can contribute to the transition towards sustainable development.

2. These new behaviors should be developed and practiced in the immediate environment of the school through democratic, progressive, and dynamic activities based on praxis. This results in a tangible reduction of the school's own environmental impact.

3. The key concept is that environmental education should be incorporated into formal education policies and programs in a planned and strategic manner, rather than relying on individual commitment or enthusiasm.

The second benefit demonstrates the coherence between the curricular approach to environmental education and its practical implementation. This means aligning what is taught in the classroom with what is experienced by both students and teachers throughout the school environment.

As described above, the school plays a crucial role in the development and implementation of environmental education. Environmental education is an educational approach that aims to change paradigms on the path towards sustainable development. In this context, the school should not only be an agent of change but also be seen as an object of change itself. It becomes a place for the practical application of new values fostered by environmental education.

Through environmental education, schools are responsible for awakening in citizens a critical awareness about the environment, recognizing it as a common good, a natural right, and essential to life. The essence of education lies in the development of both content and praxis, fostering a dialectical relationship between environmental issues and societal engagement. This process aims to cultivate changes in attitudes that students learn at school and subsequently apply in their social and family environments.

11. ENVIRONMENTAL EDUCATION AND POPULAR PARTICIPATION

The preservation of the environment depends on everyone: government, educators, companies, non-governmental organizations (NGOs), media, and every citizen. Environmental education is fundamental in solving these problems, as it will encourage citizens to know and do their part, including: avoiding waste of water, electricity, and unnecessary consumption; selective collection; purchasing products from companies concerned about the environment; demanding that competent authorities enforce the law; treating garbage and sewage correctly; protecting natural areas; making land use plans; and encouraging recycling, among others.

Environmental education emphasizes local norms, and seeks to maintain respect for the different ecosystems and human cultures of Earth. The duty to recognize global similarities, while effectively interacting with local specifics, is summarized in the following motto: Think globally, act locally.

An environmental education program, to be effective, must simultaneously promote the development of knowledge, attitudes, and skills necessary for the preservation and improvement of environmental quality. We start small, with the school as a laboratory, understanding urban metabolism and its use of natural and physical resources. We expand through the surrounding area and successively to the city, region, country, continent, and planet.

Environmental education is a comprehensive form of education, which aims to reach all citizens, through a permanent participatory pedagogical process that seeks to instill critical awareness about environmental problems, providing an overview of the genesis and evolution of today's environmental problems.

Learning is always more effective if the activity is adapted to the real life situations of the particular environment in which students and teachers live.

In 1975, as an offshoot of the Stockholm Conference, the International Seminar on Environmental Education took place in Belgrade, where the conceptual bases of environmental education were defined. Guimarães (1995) made the following statement:

"The basic principle of environmental education is attention to the natural and artificial environment, considering ecological, political, social, cultural, and aesthetic factors. Environmental education should be continuous, multidisciplinary, integrated within regional differences, focused on national interests, and focused on questioning the type of development. Its priority goal is the formation in individuals of a collective consciousness, capable of discerning the environmental importance in the preservation of the human species and, above all, stimulating cooperative behavior in different inter- and intra-nation relations."

As a social movement, the environmental issue consolidated in the late 1960s and in the early

1970s. But it has been only since the 1980s that it became popularized.

Guimarães (1995) points out that it is necessary to exercise praxis in environmental education, because only action generates activism. Study alone generates inaction that will not fulfill the transformative possibility of education. Thus, the solution would be to participate in a true dialogue between the reflexive attitude and the action of theory with practice, that is, thinking with doing. This process strengthens human knowledge and enables us to alter our destiny.

The following quote by Freire (1983) seems very appropriate to this concept:

> "Man is a being of relationships. Culture is a reflection of man's creative process, and this creative process makes him an agent of active adaptation and not of accommodation. This conception distinguishes nature from culture, understanding culture as the result of his work, of his creative effort. This discovery is responsible for the rescue of self-esteem, because, just as culture is the work of a

great sculptor, so is the brick made by the potter. We try to overcome the dichotomy between theory and practice, because during the process, when man discovers that his practice supposes knowledge, he concludes that knowing is interfering in reality; he perceives himself as a subject of history."

For education, including environmental education, to be effective, it cannot be something imposed through the educator-student model. Rather, it must be reflective, and constructed, as Freire (1983) has stated.

Some concepts used frequently in environmental education are not always understood in their full meaning and generate serious conceptual problems in developing critical thinking. The following are some of them:

It is necessary that the process of environmental education is carried out with real, active participation of the students. Brugger (1994) defines what does not constitute genuine education: a type of instruction where people are led to perform a certain type of function or task, identified with a certain utilitarian, one-dimensional pattern of thought-action. It is ineffective for aspirations and objectives, which by their content transcend the established universe of word and action, and are reduced to terms of that universe.

According to Jacobi (1999), to carry out an education process, whether environmental or not, it is necessary to create a concept of general interest that is strengthened incrementally. As the dimensions of education for active citizenship are absorbed, the effect will be the multiplication of participation in the decisive processes of public interest.

In this view, the process of participation is only realized through conscious acceptance of its purpose and access to information. Only through inclusiveness, especially of more excluded social groups, can we promote the behavioral changes necessary to enable more action oriented toward the common good. Well-informed citizens, by recognizing themselves as relevant actors, are more able to pressure authorities, as well as to motivate themselves for actions of co-responsibility and community participation (Jacobi, 1999).

It is necessary to organize and formulate strategies based on participatory processes, between governmental organizations and NGOs. This is the only way to maintain socio-political commitment aimed at achieving environmental management objectives, particularly by including the most deprived strata of the population.

Based on this process, Jacobi (1999) explains that the need to strengthen the institutional context is unquestionable. Jacobi argues that for this to occur, it is essential to generate references for residents regarding the availability, access, and costs of services locally. This will allow them to establish various links with the perception of environmental problems in their most immediate surroundings, neighborhood, and home.

The existing challenge is to formulate viable approaches for the implementation of improvements that are both technically and socially efficient. Institutional strengthening is a relevant but not sufficient condition to consolidate improvements. There is a need to take into account the level of information and/or misinformation of residents about interrelations between the environment and their involvement and motivations with a perspective that emphasizes the general interest (Jacobi, 1999).

Institutional reforms and, fundamentally, new methods in the processes of managing environmental issues will be important for the success of environmental policies (Cahn, 1995). Considering this possibility, there is an urgent need for the adoption of educational measures that are directed toward the betterment of the environment. We must not forget that humans have been making decisions affecting the environment for millennia, and evaluating the impact has not always been balanced.

Paradigm shifts require changes in attitude (Loureiro et al., 2002). Environmental education seeks to implement new relationships between humans and other species, humans with the abiotic environment, and most importantly, between humans and other humans.

The scope of environmental education must be comprehensive, beginning within households and expanding through local communities, urban centers, and marginalized areas. It should address poverty concentration, challenge oppressive systems, embrace regional particularities and cultural diversity, ultimately connecting local environmental concerns with national environmental policies. The basic aim of environmental education is to ensure a healthy environment for all humans and all types of life existing on the face of the Earth.

Freire (2002) develops educational praxis through dialectics. This is a process of reflection and action in the construction of knowledge; it is a fundamental way to intervene in reality and promote change leading to citizenship. This implies a back-and-forth movement between the critical understanding of reality and the transformative social action. All this is based on the principle that human beings educate themselves mutually, mediated by the observable world.

Loureiro et al. (2002) state that environmental education is an educational and social praxis that aims to construct values, concepts, skills, and attitudes that enable the understanding of the reality of life, plus the lucid and responsible action of individual and collective social actors on the environment. In this sense, it contributes to the attempt to implement a civilizational and societal pattern distinct from the current one, based on a new ethics of the relationship between society and nature. Thus, for the real transformation of the structural and conjunctural matrix in which we live, environmental education, by definition, is a strategic element in the formation of broad critical awareness of social and production relations that balance human needs and nature.

Environmental education, understood as learning new skills that lead to changing values and attitudes, in search of new thinking and acting for the benefit of future generations, should involve all who interact with the environment: the production sector, government, and organized civil society.

12. TOWARD A TRANSFORMATIVE FUTURE: ENVIRONMENTAL EDUCATION AS CATALYST FOR GLOBAL CHANGE

As we reach the conclusion of this exploration into environmental education as a new learning pathway, we find ourselves at a critical juncture in human history. The convergence of environmental crisis, educational transformation, and social awakening presents both unprecedented challenges and remarkable opportunities for creating a more sustainable and equitable world.

Throughout this book, we have examined how environmental education transcends traditional pedagogical boundaries to become a transformative force that integrates scientific knowledge, social consciousness, and ethical responsibility. From our discussion of the teaching-learning relationship in Chapter 1 to our exploration of popular participation in Chapter 11, a clear pattern emerges: environmental education is not merely about imparting knowledge of ecological systems, but about fostering a fundamental shift in how we understand our relationship with the natural world and with each other.

The paradigmatic crisis we explored in Chapter 2 reveals the inadequacy of our current economic and social development models. The Cartesian paradigm, as discussed in Chapter 3, has created a mechanistic worldview that separates humans from nature and perpetuates exploitative relationships. However, environmental education offers a pathway toward a new paradigm based on interconnection, complexity, and holistic understanding. This paradigm recognizes that environmental problems are fundamentally social problems, requiring solutions that address both ecological degradation and social inequality.

Our examination of educational policies in Chapter 4 demonstrates that systemic change requires more than individual awareness; it demands institutional transformation and policy reform. The sustainability policies discussed in Chapter 5 show

how governance structures must evolve to support long-term environmental health rather than short-term economic gains. These policy frameworks become effective only when supported by an educated citizenry capable of critical reflection and democratic participation.

The principles of adult learning explored in Chapter 6 reveal that environmental education must adapt to diverse learning contexts and acknowledge the rich experiential knowledge that individuals bring to the learning process. This approach, grounded in andragogical principles and constructivist theory, recognizes that adults learn most effectively when education connects to their lived experiences and empowers them to take meaningful action in their communities.

Chapter 7's definition of environmental education as a pathway emphasizes its role in establishing cause-and-effect relationships between ecological degradation and social systems. This understanding moves beyond simple conservation messages to address the underlying drivers of environmental crisis. The historical perspective provided in Chapter 8 shows how environmental education has evolved alongside global environmental consciousness, from the Stockholm Conference of 1972 through the recent COP conferences, reflecting humanity's growing awareness of our planetary interconnectedness.

The critical reflection explored in Chapter 9 demonstrates how environmental education becomes most powerful when it generates praxis, the dynamic cycle of action, reflection, and renewed action. This approach transforms environmental education from passive knowledge consumption to active engagement with environmental and social justice issues. Such critical environmental education recognizes that genuine sustainability cannot be achieved without addressing structural inequalities and power imbalances.

Chapter 10's focus on environmental education in schools highlights the crucial role of formal education systems in shaping environmental consciousness. Schools serve as laboratories for sustainable practices and spaces where students can experience the integration of environmental awareness with daily life. However, effective school-based environmental education requires more than curriculum changes; it demands a complete transformation of educational culture and practice.

Finally, Chapter 11's emphasis on popular participation reveals that environmental education reaches its full potential only when it becomes a tool for democratic engagement and collective action. Environmental challenges require collective responses, and environmental education must foster the collaborative skills and shared consciousness necessary for effective environmental stewardship.

The climate crisis, biodiversity loss, and environmental injustice we face today demand nothing less than a fundamental transformation in how we educate, how we relate to nature, and how we organize society. Environmental education, as presented throughout this book, offers a framework for this transformation. It provides the conceptual tools, pedagogical approaches, and ethical foundations necessary for creating a more sustainable world.

This transformation begins with recognizing that environmental education is inherently political. It challenges existing power structures, questions dominant economic paradigms, and advocates for the rights of marginalized communities who disproportionately bear the burden of environmental degradation. Environmental education that avoids these political dimensions fails to address the root causes of environmental crisis and inadvertently perpetuates the systems that created our current challenges.

The concept of praxis, the integration of critical reflection and transformative action, serves as the cornerstone of truly effective environmental education. This approach moves beyond awareness-raising to engage learners in real-world environmental problem-solving and social change efforts. Students become researchers, advocates, and change agents rather than passive recipients of environmental information.

Environmental education as praxis recognizes that learning occurs through engagement with authentic environmental challenges in local communities. Students investigate pollution sources, participate in habitat restoration, engage in environmental policy advocacy, and work with community organizations to address environmental injustices. Through these experiences, they develop both the analytical skills to understand complex environmental systems and the practical skills necessary for effective environmental action.

This approach also acknowledges that environmental problems cannot be solved through technical solutions alone. They require social and political solutions that address underlying patterns of consumption, production, and distribution. Environmental education as praxis helps learners understand these connections and develop the capacity to work for systemic change rather than merely individual behavior modification.

Environmental education, understood as a transformative practice, aims to develop what we might call "ecological citizens," individuals who understand their embeddedness within ecological systems and their responsibility to work for environmental and social justice. These ecological citizens demonstrate systems thinking by understanding the interconnections between environmental, social, and economic systems and analyzing environmental problems from multiple perspectives. They possess critical consciousness that enables them to identify and challenge the structural causes of environmental degradation, including patterns of inequality and injustice. Their democratic engagement allows them to participate effectively in environmental decision-making processes and work collaboratively with diverse stakeholders. Through cultural competency, they recognize and respect diverse ways of knowing and relating to the natural world, including indigenous and traditional ecological knowledge systems. Finally, their action competence enables them to translate environmental understanding into effective action, whether through individual lifestyle changes, community organizing, policy advocacy, or professional practice.

Environmental educators play a crucial role in fostering this transformation. Rather than simply transmitting environmental information, they serve as facilitators of critical inquiry, community organizers, and catalysts for social change. Effective environmental educators understand that their work is inherently political and ethical. They help learners develop the capacity to analyze environmental problems critically and to take action for environmental and social justice.

This requires environmental educators to develop new competencies beyond traditional teaching skills. They must understand environmental justice issues, be familiar with community organizing strategies, and possess the skills to facilitate difficult conversations about controversial environmental topics. They must also be prepared to support learners in taking action, even when that action challenges existing institutional practices or power structures.

Individual transformation, while necessary, is insufficient to address the scale and urgency of environmental challenges. Environmental education must also work to transform the institutions within which it operates. Schools, universities, community organizations, and government agencies must align their practices with environmental values and become models of sustainability.

This institutional transformation involves multiple dimensions that work together to create comprehensive change. Educational institutions must reduce their environmental footprint through energy efficiency, waste reduction, sustainable transportation, and responsible procurement practices in their operational approaches. Environmental perspectives must be integrated across all areas of study rather than confined to specialized environmental courses through comprehensive curriculum integration. These institutions must engage actively with local communities to address environmental challenges and support community-led environmental initiatives through meaningful community engagement. They have a responsibility to advocate for policies that support environmental protection and social justice through active policy advocacy. Research institutions must prioritize the investigation of environmental problems and solutions, with particular attention to community-based and participatory research approaches in their research priorities.

Environmental education must balance global awareness with local action. Students need to understand global environmental challenges such as climate change, biodiversity loss, and ocean acidification. However, this global awareness must be connected to local environmental conditions and opportunities for action. The motto "think globally, act locally" remains relevant, but it must be understood as a call to connect local action to global environmental justice movements.

This approach recognizes that environmental problems manifest differently in different places and that solutions must be adapted to local ecological, cultural, and economic conditions. Environmental education helps learners understand these place-based dimensions while also recognizing common patterns and shared challenges across different contexts.

Digital technologies offer new opportunities for environmental education, including virtual field experiences, global collaboration on environmental projects, and access to real-time environmental data. However, environmental educators must approach these technologies critically, recognizing their environmental costs and ensuring that they enhance rather than replace direct experience with natural systems.

The most effective uses of technology in environmental education support community-based environmental monitoring, facilitate collaboration between diverse stakeholders, and provide access to environmental information for marginalized communities. Technology should be used to democratize environmental knowledge and support environmental justice rather than to create new forms of digital divide.

Traditional approaches to educational evaluation, focused on knowledge acquisition and individual behavior change, are inadequate for assessing the impact of transformative environmental education. New evaluation approaches must examine collective outcomes, institutional changes, and contributions to environmental and social justice movements.

Effective evaluation of environmental education must consider multiple indicators that reflect its transformative potential. Individual outcomes include changes in environmental knowledge, attitudes, and behaviors, as well as development of critical thinking and action competencies. Collective outcomes encompass the formation of environmental organizations, participation in environmental policy processes, and contributions to community environmental initiatives. Institutional changes are evidenced through the adoption of sustainable practices, integration of environmental perspectives across organizational functions, and support for environmental and social justice initiatives. Environmental improvements can be measured through local environmental conditions such as air and water quality, biodiversity conservation, and waste reduction. Social justice outcomes are demonstrated through the reduction of environmental health disparities, increased participation of marginalized communities in environmental decision-making, and advancement of environmental justice policies.

Environmental education stands at a crossroads. We can continue with approaches that focus primarily on individual awareness and behavior change, achieving modest improvements while failing to address the fundamental drivers of environmental crisis. Alternatively, we can embrace environmental education as a transformative practice that develops ecological citizens capable of working for systemic change.

The path forward requires courage to challenge existing educational practices, institutional structures, and social arrangements that perpetuate environmental destruction. It demands that we recognize environmental education as inherently political and ethical work that must address issues of power, justice, and democracy. It requires that we support environmental educators in developing the knowledge, skills, and institutional support necessary for transformative practice.

Most importantly, the path forward requires that we maintain hope in the face of overwhelming environmental challenges. Environmental education, understood as a practice of freedom, offers a pathway toward a more just and sustainable world. Through critical reflection, collaborative action, and unwavering commitment to both environmental protection and social justice, environmental education can serve as a catalyst for the transformation our world urgently needs.

Environmental education represents far more than a pedagogical approach or curricular addition. It embodies a fundamental reimagining of education's role in society and a pathway toward the radical transformation necessary to address our environmental and social crises. Through the integration of critical reflection and transformative action, environmental education has the potential to develop ecological citizens capable of creating a more just and sustainable world.

The journey outlined in this book, from understanding the relationship between teaching and learning to fostering popular participation in environmental protection, reveals environmental education's transformative potential. However, realizing this potential requires that we approach environmental education as inherently political work that must address the structural causes of environmental destruction while building the democratic capacity necessary for genuine sustainability.

As we face an uncertain environmental future, environmental education offers not just hope but a concrete pathway for action. By fostering critical environmental consciousness, supporting community-based environmental initiatives, and working to transform educational institutions, environmental education can serve as a powerful catalyst for the social and ecological transformation our world desperately needs.

The new learning pathway we have explored in this book is not simply an educational innovation but an essential component of humanity's response to the environmental crisis. Through environmental education that embraces its transformative potential, we can work together to create a world where human communities and natural systems thrive in dynamic balance, where environmental protection and social justice advance together, and where education serves as a practice of freedom for all Earth's inhabitants.

The future of environmental education, and indeed the future of our planet, depends on our willingness to embrace this transformative vision and work tirelessly to make it a reality. The path forward is challenging, but the stakes could not be higher.

Environmental education as a new learning pathway offers not just hope for a better future, but a concrete strategy for creating it.

ABOUT THE AUTHOR

Dr. Barbara Lobo is an educator and environmental scientist who bridges science and education. Born in Brazil and living in the United States since 2016, she holds a Post-doctorate and Doctorate in Education Sciences and a Master's in Health Sciences and Environment.

With over 15 years in higher education, Dr. Lobo previously taught at Universidade Estácio de Sá in Brazil and currently teaches at Southern New Hampshire University in USA. She has authored multiple books on environmental science, education, and personal development.

Coming from a literary family—daughter of writer Izabel Monteiro and granddaughter of Athos Fernandes Monteiro—Dr. Lobo combines academic expertise with a passion for writing. Mother of Luiza and Gabriel, grandmother of Tyler and Mia, and wife of Alberto Lobo, she believes education should integrate scientific knowledge with personal growth to create a more sustainable world.

Connect with Dr. Barbara Lobo:

- **Email:** barbaralobo.writer@gmail.com
- **LinkedIn:** Barbara Lobo, PhD
- **Instagram:**
  @dr.barbara_lobo | @barbaralobo.phd

REFERENCES

Almino, J. (1993). *Naturezas mortas: A filosofia política do ecologismo*. Fundação Alexandre Gusmão.

Alves, R. C. (2020). *A (in)viabilidade de consórcios públicos intermunicipais para a gestão de resíduos sólidos no amazonas* [Master's thesis, Universidade Federal do Amazonas].

Andrade, P. G. G. (2017). *O meio ambiente nos tribunais internacionais: Diálogo de jurisdições e unidade do sistema jurídico* [Master's thesis, Universidade Federal de Minas Gerais].

Amorim, P., & Lobo, B. (2016). *Ambiente econômico e aprendizagem*. Autografia.

Amorim, P., & Lobo, B. (2019). *Corrupção, ambiente econômico e aprendizagem*. Amazon.

Barbieri, J. C. (1997). *Desenvolvimento e meio ambiente*. Vozes.

BBC Brazil News. (2021). Os quinze países que mais emitiram CO2 nos últimos 20 anos. Retrieved from https://www.bbc.com/portuguese/brasil-50811386.amp

Belchior, G. P. N., & Matias, J. L. N. (2011). O princípio da solidariedade como marco jurídico-constitucional do Estado de direito ambiental. In M. L. Hauschild, J. C. Guedes, & O. L. Rodrigues Júnior (Eds.), *Meio ambiente, propriedade e agronegócio* (Vol. 1). IP Editora.

Bioscience. (2020). World scientists' warning of a climate emergency. Retrieved from https://academic.oup.com/bioscience

Blums, A. (1995). *The tension between liberalism and environmental policymaking in the United States*. State University of New York Press.

BNDES. (2014). *Análise das diversas tecnologias de tratamento e disposição final de resíduos sólidos urbanos no Brasil, Europa, Estados Unidos e Japão*. Grupo de Resíduos Sólidos - UFPE.

Boff, L. (1999). *Ecologia: Grito da terra, grito dos pobres*. Ática.

Boff, L. (2000). *Saber cuidar: Ética do humano: Compaixão pela terra*. Vozes.

Brasil, P. E. M. A. S. (2016). *A proteção do meio ambiente como dever fundamental* [Doctoral dissertation, Universidade Federal do Ceará].

Brúseke, F. J. (1996). Desestruturação e desenvolvimento. In E. Viola & L. C. Ferreira (Eds.), *Incertezas de sustentabilidade na globalização*. Unicamp.

Brugger, P. (1994). *Educação ou adestramento ambiental*. Letras Contemporâneas.

Buarque, C. (1990). *A desordem do progresso: O fim da era dos economistas e a construção do futuro*. Paz e Terra.

Cahn, M. A. (1995). *The tension between liberalism and environmental policymaking in the United States*. State University of New York Press.

Capra, F. (1982). *O ponto de mutação*. Cultrix.

Cardoso, S. B. (2016). *Desenvolvimento sustentável: Variáveis e caminhos a longo prazo* [Bachelor's thesis, Centro de Instrução Almirante Graça Aranha].

Caulley, D. N. (1981). *Document analysis in program evaluation*. Northwest Regional Educational Laboratory.

Cavalcanti, C. (2002). *Política de governo para o desenvolvimento sustentável: Uma introdução ao tema e a esta obra coletiva*. Cortez.

Cleveland, C. J. (2002). Capital humano, capital natural e limites biofísicos no processo econômico. In C. Cavalcanti, *Política de governo para o desenvolvimento sustentável: Uma introdução ao tema e a esta obra coletiva*. Cortez.

Colacios, R. D. (2014). *Um clima de incertezas: As controvérsias científicas sobre mudanças climáticas nas revistas Science e Nature (1970-2005)* [Doctoral dissertation, Universidade de São Paulo].

Constituição da República Portuguesa. (2020). Retrieved from http://www.ministeriopublico.pt/iframe/constituicao-da-republica-portuguesa

Constituição Federal do Brasil. (2020). Retrieved from http://www.jusbrasil.com.br

Correia de Andrade, M. (1994). *O desafio ecológico: Utopia e realidade*. HUCITEC.

Cozetti, N. (2001). Lixo: Marca incômoda de modernidade. *Revista Ecologia e Desenvolvimento, 96*.

Cruz, G. D. (2001). As riquezas que jogamos fora. *Revista Ecologia e Desenvolvimento, 77*, 46-51.

De Souza, R. T. (1996). *Totalidade e desagregação: Sobre as fronteiras do pensamento e suas alternativas*. EDIPUCRS.

Denninger, E. (2000). Security, diversity, solidarity instead of freedom, equality, fraternity. *Constellations, 7*(4), 507-521.

Dias, G. F. (1992). *Educação ambiental: Princípios e práticas*. Gaia.

Dias, G. F. (2002). *Pegada ecológica e sustentabilidade humana*. Gaia.

Fiorillo, C. A. P. (2004). *Curso de direito ambiental brasileiro* (5th ed.). Saraiva.

Fisher, E. (2017). *Environmental law: A very short introduction*. Oxford University Press.

Foladori, G. (2004). Um olhar antropológico sobre a questão ambiental. *MANA*, 323-348. Retrieved from http://www.scielo.br/

Forattini, O. P. (1992). *Ecologia, epidemiologia e sociedade*. Edusp.

Freire, P. (1983). *Educação e mudança* (11th ed.). Paz e Terra.

Freire, P. (2002). *Pedagogia do oprimido* (34th ed.). Paz e Terra.

Furtado, C. (1996). *O mito do desenvolvimento econômico.* Paz e Terra.

Gil, A. C. (1991). *Como elaborar projetos de pesquisa.* Atlas.

Gonçalves, C. W. P. (1990). *Os (des)caminhos do meio ambiente* (2nd ed.). Contexto.

Gonçalves, C. W. P. (2002). Natureza e sociedade: Elementos para uma ética da sustentabilidade. In J. A. A. Coimbra (Ed.), *Fronteiras da ética.* Senac.

Guba, E. G., & Lincoln, Y. S. (1981). *Effective evaluation.* Jossey-Bass.

Gudynas, E. (1992). Ética, ambiente e ecologia: Uma crise entrelaçada. *Revista Eclesiástica Brasileira, 52*(205), 68-69.

Guimarães, M. (1995). *A dimensão ambiental na educação.* Papirus.

Guimarães, R. P. (1991). Assimetria dos interesses compartilhados: América Latina e a agenda global do meio ambiente. In H. R. Leis (Ed.), *Ecologia e política mundial.* Vozes/FASE.

Herculano, S. C. (1992). Do desenvolvimento (in)suportável à sociedade feliz. In M. Goldenberg (Ed.), *Ecologia, ciência e política.* Revan.

IBGE. (2018). Estimativas de população dos municípios para 2018. Retrieved from https://agenciadenoticias.ibge.gov.br/agencia-sala-de-imprensa/2013-agencia-de-noticias/releases/22374-ibge-divulga-as-estimativas-de-populacao-dos-municipios-para-2018

Intergovernmental Panel on Climate Change. (2019). *Climate change and land.* Retrieved from https://www.ipcc.ch

Intergovernmental Panel on Climate Change. (2021). *Climate change.* Retrieved from https://www.ipcc.ch

Irving, M. A. (2003). Projeto Sana Sustentável: Uma iniciativa de base comunitária. In M. D'Ávila & R. Pedro, *Tecendo o desenvolvimento: Saberes, gênero e ecologia social.* Bapera.

Jacobi, P. (1999). *Cidade e meio ambiente: Percepções e práticas em São Paulo.* Annablume.

Jonas, H. (1995). *El principio de responsabilidad: Ensayo de una ética para la civilización tecnológica.* Herder.

La Torre, M. A. (1993). *Ecología y moral: La irrupción de la instancia ecológica en la ética de Occidente.* Editorial Desclée de Brouwer.

Lago, A., & Pádua, J. A. (1992). *O que é ecologia.* Brasiliense.

Lobo, B. (2021). *Environmental crisis: Fleeing from chaos.* Amazon Digital Services LLC - KDP.

Leis ambientais brasileiras. (2020). Retrieved from http://www.estrategiaods.org.br/as-sete-principais-leis-ambientais-brasileiras/; https://iusnatura.com.br/principais-leis-ambientais/

Lima, M. F. C. (1993). Desenvolvimento sustentável, a crise do fordismo e os países periféricos. In A. M. Rodrigues (Ed.), *Meio ambiente ecos da ECO.* Unicamp.

Loureiro, C. F. B., & Torres, J. R. (2014). *Educação ambiental dialogando com Paulo Freire.* Cortez.

Lüdke, M., & André, M. (1986). *Pesquisa em educação: Abordagens qualitativas.* E.P.U.

Machado, C. J. S. (2003). Sociedade, meio ambiente e políticas públicas e a erradicação das velhas práticas. *Jornal da Ciência.* Retrieved from http://www.jornaldaciencia.org.br

Machado, P. A. L. (2002). *Direito ambiental brasileiro* (pp. 127-128). Malheiros.

Marriott, B. B. (1997). *Environmental impact assessment: A practical guide.* United States.

Matias, J. L. N. (2013). Em busca de uma sociedade livre, justa e solidária: A função ambiental como forma de conciliação entre o direito de propriedade e o direito ao meio ambiente sadio. In J. L. Nogueira (Coord.), T. S. Sales, & A. C. B. Aguiar (Eds.), *Ordem econômica na perspectiva dos direitos fundamentais.* CRV.

137

Matias, J. L. N., & Matias, J. F. N. (2010). A convergência entre os direitos de propriedade e ao meio ambiente sadio: A cessão de uso das águas da União para a produção de pescado no Brasil. In *A efetivação do direito de propriedade para o desenvolvimento sustentável: Relatos e proposições.* Fundação Boiteux.

Matias, J. L. N., & Mattei, J. (2014). Aspectos comparativos da proteção ambiental no Brasil e na Alemanha. *Nomos: Revista do Programa de Pós-graduação em Direito da UFC, 34*(2), 227-244.

May, T. (2004). *Pesquisa social: Questões, métodos e processos* (3rd ed.). Artmed.

Meireles, S. (2001). Crimes ambientais, os ganhos dos acordos judiciais. *Revista Ecologia e Desenvolvimento, 92.*

Ministério do Meio Ambiente. (2005). Retrieved from http://www.ministeriomeioambiente.gov.br

Miranda, E. E., Dorado, A. J., & Assumpção, J. V. (1994). *Doenças respiratórias crônicas em quatro municípios paulistas.* Ecoforça.

Moreira, A. C. M. L. (2004). Conceitos de ambiente e de impacto ambiental aplicáveis ao meio urbano. Retrieved from http://www.usp.br

Morin, E., & Kern, B. (1995). *Terra-pátria.* Sulina.

Morin, E., & Terrena, M. (2001). *Saberes globais e saberes locais* (3rd ed., P. Y. Stroh, Trans.). Garamond.

Mucci, J. L. N. (2005). *Introdução às ciências ambientais.* Manole.

Neiva, A., Moreira, M., Cozetti, N., Meirelles, S., Noronha, S., & Mineiro, P. (2001). Agenda 21, o futuro que o brasileiro quer. *Revista Ecologia e Desenvolvimento, 93.*

Oliveira, J. C. M. (2017). *Soft sensor veicular para emissão de medições de gases* [Master's thesis, Universidade Federal Rio Grande do Norte].

O'Neill, K. (2019). *Waste.* Cambridge University Press.

Pacifici, M., Foden, W. B., Visconti, P., Watson, J. E. M., Butchart, S. H. M., et al. (2015). Assessing species vulnerability to climate change. *Nature Climate Change.*

Peccei, A., & Ikeda, D. (1984). *Antes que seja tarde demais.* Record.

Pelicioni, A. F. (2005). *O movimento ambientalista e a educação ambiental.* Manole.

Philippi Jr., A. (Ed.). (1988). *Saneamento do meio.* Fundacentro.

Philippi Jr., A., & Malheiros, T. F. (2005). *Saúde ambiental e desenvolvimento.* USP.

População mundial. (2019). Relatório da ONU em 2019. Retrieved from https://nacoesunidas.org/populacao-mundial-deve-chegar-a-97-bilhoes-de-pessoas-em-2050-diz-relatorio-da-onu/amp/#

Roegen, G. (1971). *The entropy law and the economic process*. Harvard University Press.

Sachs, I. (1986). *Ecodesenvolvimento: Crescer sem destruir*. Vértice.

Sachs, J. D. (2015). *The age of sustainable development*. Columbia University Press.

Santos, A. R. (2005). *Climatologia*.

Saylan, C., & Blumstein, D. T. (2011). *The failure of environmental education*. University of California Press.

Sobral, H. R., & Silva, C. C. A. (1989). Balanço sobre a situação do meio ambiente na metrópole de São Paulo. *São Paulo, Perspectivas*.

Stahel, A. W. (1995). Capitalismo e entropia: Os aspectos ideológicos de uma contradição e uma busca de alternativas sustentáveis. In C. Cavalcanti (Ed.), *Desenvolvimento e natureza: Estudos para uma sociedade sustentável*. Cortez.

Steffen, W., et al. (2018). Trajectories of the Earth System in the Anthropocene. *Proceedings of the National Academy of Sciences*.

Toynbee, A. (1974). *A sociedade do futuro* (2nd ed.). Zahar Editores.

UNEP. (2020). Consumo crescente em escala regional. Retrieved from http://www.mma.gov.br/

Vieira, P. F. (1995). Meio ambiente, desenvolvimento e planejamento. In *Meio ambiente, desenvolvimento e cidadania: Desafios para as ciências sociais*. Cortez.

Viola, E. (1996). Reflexões sobre os dilemas do Brasil na segunda metade da década de 1990 e sobre uma agenda de políticas públicas baseadas na democracia, na equidade, na eficiência e na sustentabilidade. *Anais. Meio Ambiente, desenvolvimento e política de governo – Workshop*. Fundação Joaquim Nabuco.

Viola, E., & Leis, H. (1991). Desordem global da biosfera e a nova ordem internacional: O papel organizador do ecologismo. In H. R. Leis (Ed.), *Ecologia e política mundial*. Vozes/FASE.

Viola, E., & Leis, H. (1995). A evolução das políticas ambientais no Brasil, 1971-1991: Do bissetorialismo preservacionista para o multissetorialismo orientado para o desenvolvimento sustentável. In D. Hogan & P. F. Vieira (Eds.), *Dilemas socioambientais e desenvolvimento sustentável*. Unicamp.

Vitor, C. (2002). A questão ambiental deve estar no centro de tudo. *Revista Ecologia e Desenvolvimento, 100*.

World Bank. (2020). What a waste 2.0: A global snapshot of solid waste management to 2050. Retrieved from https://openknowledge.world.org/handle/10986/2174

World Bank. (2021). CO2 emissions (kt). Retrieved from https://databank.worldbank.org

World Bank. (2021). Total greenhouse emissions (kt of CO2 equivalent). Retrieved from https://databank.worldbank.org